ARA

Collected Verses on Life

Compiled by K. H. Brady

"Then let us smile when skies are gray,
       And laugh at stormy weather,
       And sing life's lonesome times away:
So worry and the dreariest day
Will find an end together."

~ Unknown

ILLUSTRATIONS Chinese Arabesques
ARTIST Anne Allen, Jean-Baptiste Pillement
DATE ca. 1790s
From Nouvelle suite de cahiers arabesques
chinois a l'usage des dessinateurs et des peintres

THE SPRING OF LOVE

~ Stopford A. Brooks

A little sun, a little rain,
      O soft wind blowing from the West,
   And woods and fields are sweet again
     And Warmth within the mountain's breast.

A little love, a little trust,
     A soft impulse, a sudden dream,
   And life as dry as desert dust,
     Is fresher than a mountain stream.

Arabesque ~ Emma Lazarus

On a background of pale gold
I would trace with quaint design,
    Penciled fine,
Brilliant-colored, Moorish scenes,
Mosques and crescents, pages, queens,
    Line on line,
That the prose-world of to-day
Might the gorgeous Past's array
    Once behold.
On the magic painted shield
Rich Granada's Vega green
    Should be seen;
Crystal fountains, coolness flinging,
Hanging gardens' skyward springing
    Emerald sheen;
Ruddy when the daylight falls,
Crowned Alhambra's beetling walls
    Stand revealed;
Balconies that overbrow
Field and city, vale and stream.
    In a dream
Lulled the drowsy landscape basks;
    Mark the gleam
Silvery of each white-swathed peak!
Mountain-airs caress the cheek,
    Fresh from the snow.
Here in Lindaraxa's bower
The immortal roses bloom;
    In the room
Lion-guarded, marble-paven,
Still the fountain leaps to heaven.
    But the doom
Of the banned and stricken race
Overshadows every place,
    Every hour.

Where fair Lindaraxa dwelt
Flits the bat on velvet wings;
    Mute the strings
Of the broken mandoline;
The Pavilion of the Queen
    Widely flings
Vacant windows to the night;
Moonbeams kiss the floor with light
    Where she knelt.
Through these halls that people stepped
Who through darkling centuries
    Held the keys
Of all wisdom, truth, and art,
In a Paradise apart,
    Lapped in ease,
Sagely pondering deathless themes,
While, befooled with monkish dreams,
    Europe slept.
Where shall they be found today?
Yonder hill that frets the sky
    "The last Sigh
Of the Moor" is named still.
There the ill-starred Boabdil
    Bade good-by
To Granada and to Spain,
Where the Crescent ne'er again
    Holdeth sway.
Vanished like the wind that blows,
Whither shall we seek their trace
    On earth's face?
The gigantic wheel of fate,
Crushing all things soon or late,
    Now a race,
Now a single life o'erruns,
Now a universe of suns,
    Now a rose.

Crossing the Bar ~ Alfred, Lord Tennyson

Sunset and evening star,
    And one clear call for me,
    And may there be no moaning of the bar,
    When I put out to sea.

But such a tide as moving seems asleep,
    Too full for sound and foam,
    When that which drew from out the boundless deep,
    Turns again home.

Twilight and evening bell,
    And after that the dark;
    And may there be no sadness of farewell,
    When I embark.

For tho' from out our bourne of time and place,
    The flood may bear me far,
    I hope to see my Pilot face to face
    When I have crossed the bar.

BALANCING ~ Wilbur D. Nesbit

The good we meant to do—the deeds
So oft misunderstood;
The thwarted good we try to do,
And would do, if we could,
The noble deeds we set upon
And have accomplished none —
Write them—and with them credit all
The bad we have not done.

WHEN THE BIRDS GO NORTH AGAIN ~ Ella Higginson

Oh, every year hath its winter,
      And every year hath its rain—
    But a day is always coming
      When the birds go north again.

When new leaves swell in the forest,
      And grass springs green on the plain,
    And the alder's veins turn crimson—
      And the birds go north again.

Oh, every heart hath its sorrow,
      And every heart hath its pain—
    But a day is always coming
      When the birds go north again.

'Tis the sweetest thing to remember
      If courage be on the wane,
    When the cold, dark days are over—
      Why, the birds go north again.

LEAD KINDLY LIGHT ~ John Henry (Cardinal) Newman

Lead kindly light, amid the encircling gloom,
    Lead thou me on!
    The night is dark and I am far from home,
    Lead thou me on!
    Keep thou my feet; I do not ask to see
    The distant scene—one step enough for me.

I was not ever thus, nor prayed that thou
    Shouldst lead me on;
    I loved to see and choose my path, but now
    Lead thou me on!
    I loved the garish day, and, spite of fears,
    Pride ruled my will: remember not past years.

So long thy power hath blessed me, sure it still
    Will lead me on;
        O'er moor and fen, o'er crag and torrent till

The night is gone; And with the morn those angel faces smile Which I have loved long since, and lost awhile.

YOUNG AND OLD ~ Charles Kingsley

When all the world is young, lad,
    When all the trees are green;
  And every goose a swan, lad,
    And every lass a queen;
  Then hey for boot and horse, lad,
    And around the world away;
  Young blood must have its course, lad,
    And every dog his day.

When all the world is old, lad,
    And all the trees are brown;
  And all the sport is stale, lad,
    And all the wheels run down;
  Creep home and take your place there,
    The spent and maimed among;
  God grant you find one face there
    You loved when all was young.

But in the mud and scum of things
        There always, always, something sings.

~Ralph Waldo Emerson

RESOLVE

~ Charlotte Perkins Stetson

To keep my health!
        To do my work!
        To live!
    To see to it I grow and gain and give!
Never to look behind me for an hour!
To wait in weakness, and to walk in power;
But always fronting onward toward the light,
Always and always facing towards the right.
Robbed, starved, defeated, fallen, wide astray—
On, with what strength I have!
Back to the way!

SYMPATHY ~ Sir Thomas N. Talfourd

'Tis a little thing

To give a cup of water; yet its draught
Of cool refreshment, drained by fevered lips,
May give a shock of pleasure to the frame
More exquisite than when nectarean juice
Renews the life of joy in happier hours.
It is a little thing to speak a phrase
Of common comfort which by daily use
Has almost lost its sense, yet on the ear
Of him who thought to die unmourned 'twill fall
Like choicest music, fill the glazing eye
With gentle tears, relax the knotted hand
To know the bonds of fellowship again;
And shed on the departing soul a sense,
More precious than the benison of friends
About the honored deathbed of the rich,
To him who else were lonely, that another
Of the great family is near and feels.

"The summer vanishes, but soon shall come
   The glad young days of yet another year.
   So do not mourn the passing of a joy,
   But rather wait the coming of a good,
   And know God never takes a gift away
   But He sends other gifts to take its place."

   ~ Unknown

THE INEVITABLE

~ Sarah Knowles Bolton

I like the man who faces what he must
    With step triumphant and a heart of cheer;
    Who fights the daily battle without fear;
    Sees his hopes fail, yet keeps unfaltering trust
    That God is God—that somehow, true and just
    His plans work out for mortals; not a tear
    Is shed when fortune, which the world holds dear,
    Falls from his grasp—better, with love, a crust
    Than living in dishonor; envies not,
    Nor loses faith in man; but does his best,
    Nor ever murmurs at his humbler lot;
    But, with a smile and words of hope, gives zest
    To every toiler. He alone is great
    Who by a life heroic conquers fate.

TIMES GO BY TURNS

~ Robert Southwell

The lopped tree in time may grow again,
    Most naked plants renew both fruit and flower;
The sorriest wight may find release of pain,
    The driest soil suck in some moistening shower;
Time goes by turns, and chances change by course,
    From foul to fair, from better hap to worse.

The sea of Fortune doth not ever flow;
    She draws her favors to the lowest ebb;
Her tides have equal times to come and go;
    Her loom doth weave the fine and coarsest web;
No joy so great but runneth to an end,
    No hap so hard but may in time amend.

Not always fall of leaf, nor ever Spring;
    Not endless night, yet not eternal

day;
The saddest birds a season find to sing;
   The roughest storm a calm may soon allay.
Thus, with succeeding turns God tempereth all,
   That man may hope to rise, yet fear to fall.

A chance may win that by mischance was lost,
   That net that holds no great takes little fish;
In some things all, in all things none are crost;
   Few all they need, but none have all they wish.
Unmingled joys here to no man befall;
   Who least, hath some; who most, hath never all.

THE ROSARY ~ Unknown

"The hours I spent with thee, dear heart,
    Are as a string of pearls to me;
I count them over, ev'ry one apart,
    My rosary; my rosary.

"Each hour a pearl, each pearl a prayer,
    To still a heart in absence wrung;
I tell each bead unto the end, and there
    A cross is hung!

"O memories that bless and burn!
    O barren gain and bitter loss!
    I kiss each bead, and strive at last to learn
    To kiss the cross ... to kiss the cross."

THE SPLENDOR FALLS

~ Alfred, Lord Tennyson

The splendor falls on castle walls
    And snowy summits old in story;
  The long light shakes across the lakes
    And the wild cataract leaps in glory,
  Blow, bugle, blow, set the wild echoes flying,
  Blow, bugle; answer, echoes, dying, dying, dying.

O hark! O hear! how thin and clear,
    And thinner, clearer, farther going!
  O sweet and far from cliff and scar
    The horns of Elfland faintly blowing!
  Blow, let us hear the purple glens replying;
  Blow, bugle; answer, echoes, dying, dying, dying.

O love, they die in yon rich sky,
    They faint on hill or field or river;
  Our echoes roll from soul to soul,
    And grow forever and forever,
  Blow, bugle, blow, set the wild echoes

flying,
And answer, echoes, answer, dying dying dying.

The quality of mercy is not strained;
> It droppeth as the gentle rain from heaven
> Upon the earth beneath; it is twice blessed;
> It blesseth him that gives and him that takes.

~ William Shakespeare

We just shake hands at meeting
        With many that come nigh;
    We nod the head in greeting
        To many that go by—

But welcome through the gateway
        Our old friends and true;

Then hearts leap up, and straightway
        There's open house for you,
      Old friends,
    There's open house for you!

~ Gerald Massey

If I can stop one heart from breaking,
    I shall not live in vain.
    If I can ease one life the aching,
    Or cool one pain,
Or help one fainting robin
    Into his nest again
I shall not live in vain.
I shall not live in vain.

~ Emily Dickinson

A PSALM OF LIFE

~ H. W. Longfellow

Tell me not in mournful numbers
    Life is but an empty dream,
For the soul is dead that slumbers,
    And things are not what they seem.

Life is real! Life is earnest!
    And the grave is not its goal;
Dust thou art, to dust returnest,
    Was not spoken of the soul.

Not enjoyment, and not sorrow,
    Is our destined end or way;
But to act, that each to-morrow
    Find us farther than to-day.

Art is long and Time is fleeting,
    And our hearts, though stout and brave,
Still, like muffled drums, are beating
    Funeral marches to the grave.

In the world's broad field of battle,
    In the bivouac of Life,
Be not like dumb, driven cattle!
    Be a hero in the strife

Trust no future, howe'er pleasant!
        Let the dead Past bury its dead!
        Act—act in the living present!
        Heart within and God o'erhead.

Lives of great men all remind us
        We can make our lives sublime,
        And, departing, leave behind us
        Footprints on the sands of time.

Footprints, that perhaps another,
        Sailing o'er life's solemn main,
        A forlorn and shipwrecked brother,
        Seeing, shall take heart again.

Let us, then be up and doing,
        With a heart for any fate;
        Still achieving, still pursuing,
        Learn to labor and to wait.

Though to-day may not fulfill
      All thy hopes, have patience still;
      For perchance to-morrow's sun
      Sees thy happier day begun.

    ~ P. Gerhardt

All is of God that is, or is to be,
>   And God is good.

> ~ John G. Whittier

Who looks to heaven alone to save his soul
>   May keep the path, but will not reach the goal:
>   But he who walks in love may wander far,
>   And God will bring him where the blessed are.

> ~ Henry Van Dyke

FORBEARANCE

~ Ralph Waldo Emerson

Hast thou named all the birds without a gun?
    Loved the wild-rose, and left it on its stalk?
    At rich men's tables eaten bread and pulse?
    Unarmed, faced danger with a heart of trust?
    And loved so well a high behavior,
    In man or maid, that thou from speech refrained,
    Nobility more nobly to repay?
    O, be my friend, and teach me to be thine!

THE LOOM OF YEARS ~
Alfred Noyes

In the light of the silent stars that shine on the struggling sea,
In the weary cry of the wind and the whisper of flower and tree,
Under the breath of laughter, deep in the tide of tears,
I hear the Loom of the Weaver that weaves the Web of Years.
The leaves of the winter wither and sink in the forest mould
To colour the flowers of April with purple and white and gold:
Light and scent and music die and are born again
In the heart of a grey-haired woman who wakes in a world of pain.
The hound, the fawn and the hawk, and the doves that croon and coo,
We are all one woof of the weaving and the one warp threads us through,
One flying cloud on the shuttle that carries our hopes and fears
As it goes thro' the Loom of the Weaver that weaves the Web of Years.
The crosiers of the fern, and the crown, the crown of the rose,

Pass with our hearts to the Silence where the wings of music close,
Pass and pass to the Timeless that never a moment mars,
Pass and pass to the Darkness that made the suns and stars.

Has the soul gone out in the Darkness? Is the dust sealed from sight?
Ah, hush, for the woof of the ages returns thro' the warp of the night!
Never that shuttle loses one thread of our hopes and fears,
As It comes thro' the Loom of the Weaver that weaves the Web of Years.
O, woven in one wide Loom thro' the throbbing weft of the whole,
One in spirit and flesh, one in body and soul,
The leaf on the winds of autumn, the bird in its hour to die,
The heart in its muffled anguish, the sea in its mournful cry,
One with the flower of a day, one with the withered moon,
One with the granite mountains that melt into the noon,
One with the dream that triumphs beyond the light of the spheres,
We come from the Loom of the Weaver that weaves the Web of Years.

AT NIGHTFALL

~ Charles Harrison Towne

I need so much the quiet of your love
        After the day's loud strife;
    I need your calm—all other things above
        After the stress of life.

I crave the haven that in your dear heart lies,
        After all toil is done;
    I need the star-shine of your heavenly eyes,
        After the day's great sun.

PIPPA'S SONG ~ Robert Browning

The year's at the spring
      And day's at the morn;
      Morning's at seven;
      The hillside's dew-pearled;
      The lark's on the wing;
      The snail's on the thorn;
      God's in his heaven—
      All's right with the world.

MY CREED ~ Alice Cary

I hold that Christian grace abounds
        Where charity is seen; that when
    We climb to heaven 'tis on the rounds
        Of love to men.

I hold all else named piety
        A selfish scheme, a vain pretense;
    Where center is not—can there be
        Circumference?

This I moreover hold, and dare
        Affirm where'er my ryme may go—
    Whatever things be sweet or fair
        Love makes them so.

Whether it be the lullabies
        That charm to rest the nursling bird,
    Or the sweet confidence of sighs
        And blushes, made without a word.

Whether the dazzling and the flush
        Of softly sumptuous garden bowers,
    Or by some cabin door a bush
        Of ragged flowers.

'Tis not the wide phylactery,
        Nor stubborn fast, nor stated prayers,
     That makes us saints; we judge the tree
        By what it bears.

And when a man can live apart
        From works, on theologic trust,
   I know the blood about his heart
        Is dry as dust.

Made in the USA
Columbia, SC
15 May 2025

57962090R00024